H V A R
STARI GRAD, VRBOSKA, JELSA

**A NEW TITLE IN THE SERIES
POCKET GUIDES FOR TOURISTS**

Number 15

Editorial Board:

Anuška Novaković
Mato Njavro
Rina Tropan
Katarina Milanović
Jure Amižić
Vlasta Matijević
Ana Ivelja
Zora Martić
Željko Blažević

Art layout:

Pero Krilanović

Map and city plans:

Ante Zidić

Proof reader:

Ana Ivelja

For the publisher:

Anuška Novaković, director

HVAR
STARI GRAD, VRBOSKA, JELSA

Text:

Niko Duboković Nadalini

Translator:

Karla Cizelj

Photographs:

Milan Babić
Tošo Dabac
Đuro Griesbach
Ivo Houška
Milan Pavić
Antun Tasovac

Publisher:

Turistkomerc, Zagreb, Ilica 26/1
Zagreb, 1974.

HVAR — the island of heather, sunshine and crickets

— the island of lavender, sage and wine

— the island of rosemary and secluded coves

Hvar is always attractive: gay and radiant in the summer — quiet and sunny in the winter. Because of its pleasant Mediterranean climate and rich vegetation the island has long been known as the Yugoslav Madeira. Due to its warm winters, which are particularly suitable for the treatment of asthmatic and various other ailments, the name Hvar has become synonymous with a warm, pleasant, healthy spring in mid-winter. Palms, aloes, pine trees, laurel, rosemary and lavender refreshen the peaceful coves and islets filling them with a multitude of pleasant scents.

Since the mid-19th century when the tourist trade began to develop in this beautiful island Hvar has been attracting new visitors every year while its old friends have never forgotten it. Whoever experiences the attractions and sunny beauty of winter in Hvar will always long to renew the experience. No wonder then that Hvar attracts visitors not only from Yugoslavia but also from many foreign countries who having once discovered it have become attached to it for ever. For them Hvar has become a second home where they spend every winter, and when they return to their homes they remember it with nostalgia looking forward to the next winter when they will pay it yet another visit.

GEO-PHYSICAL CHARACTERISTICS

Hvar (68 km long), after Cres the longest Adriatic island, is also the fourth largest in area (300 sq. m). The longitudinal road which links the town of Hvar with Sućurje at the eastern end of the island is 84 km long. The high plateau between St. Nicholas hill (626 m) and Hum (603 m) which extends from Sv. Nedjelja to Jelsa and is partly under pine woods and partly under arable land is marked by distinctive beauty and a fresh climate. The flat part of the island between Stari Grad, Vrboska and Jelsa is under vineyards which produce up to 50,000 hectolitres of wine per year.

The mildness of Hvar's climate is universally so well known that it need not be specially described. However, the climate is not the same in all parts of the island. While the town of Hvar and the southern coast of the island are more exposed to the sun and thus ideally suited for holidays in winter, the northern and more wooded side has a fresher climate and is thus better suited for summer holidays.

The town of Hvar (which has had a meteorological station ever since 1858) has an average air temperature of 8.3° Centigrade in January, 8.8° in February, 10.5° in March, 13.8° in April, 18.1° in May, 22.2° in June, 24.9° in July, 24.4° in August, 21.4° in September, 16.9° in October, 13.4° in November and 10.0° in December, and a mean annual temperature of 16.1° Centigrade.

According to meteorological studies snowfalls may be expected only during the first three months of the year and on an average of only one day per year, but the snow will not keep longer than half a day and in most cases it melts before reaching the ground.

COMMUNICATION LINKS

The island of Hvar has regular daily ship and ferry-boat links with the mainland and other islands, good bus and coach services, and occasional services by hydrofoil during the main season.

By ship
Hvar, Korčula, Dubrovnik or Split, Zadar and Rijeka — daily from 1 May till 15 October.

By ferry-boat
Hvar (Vira) — Split daily
Stari Grad — Split daily
Jelsa, Bol, Milna, Bobovišće — Split daily
Sućuraj — Drvenik 3—8 times daily

By coach
Stari Grad — Jelsa — Sućuraj — Drvenik — Makarska — Split — daily
Sarajevo — Hvar — Sarajevo — twice a week during the season

By hidrofoil
Hvar — Jelsa — Split and back — occasional services during the main season

ECONOMIC BASIS

Apart from wine-growing, which is the main branch of the island's economy, the inhabitants are concerned with the rearing of livestock (famous Hvar lamb), the growing of aromatic plants (lavender, rosemary), olives and figs, and fishing which, due to the rich fishing grounds, has always been an important local industry.

However, Hvar as a whole owes its prosperity to shipping. Although restricted in tonnage until the fall of the Venetian Republic, the island's small fleet provided a living for a large number of its urban and rural population. The first large ocean-going vessel to appear in Hvar after the fall of the Venetian Republic was used for the transport of wheat from Black Sea ports and the export of local products, primarily salted fish. Thus despite its well developed agriculture the island of Hvar owed its living and prosperity to shipping, which also provided the basis for the island's cultural development.

Before the second half of the 19th century Hvar had no regular land or sea communications, people relying on the occasional small vessel. In the interior of the island there existed only the old Illyrian, Greek and Roman roads recorded in the statute of 1331, for the island had derived no benefit from the road construction projects of the Napoleonic era.

Hvar obtained its first regular shipping link with the mainland in the 1850s, and its first regular daily service at the beginning of the 20th century. The first road sections (Jelsa — Pitve — Vrisnik and Hvar — Brusje) also date from the beginning of this century.

After the liberation at the end of the Second World War the island began to develop at a rapid rate. Electricity has since been brought to every village in the island and may new roads have been completed including the longitudinal road (84 km) which links the town of Hvar with Sućuraj at the eastern end of the island. The town of Hvar now has a new water-supply system, the construction of which included a tunnel of 1,400 m, — the longest road tunnel in Yugoslavia. Sućuraj in the east, Stari Grad in the centre, and the town of Hvar (via Vira, its northern harbour) are connected with the mainland by regular ferry-boat services. Apart from the fast motor ships which link Hvar with all major centres along the Adriatic coast the towns of Hvar and Jelsa are linked with Split by local shipping services. The new water-supply system which runs through the Hvar tunnel is about 30 km long and provides water for places on the southern coast between Jelsa and Hvar, and almost all places on the northern side of the island (Stari Grad, Vrboska, etc.).

HISTORY

Inhabited in prehistoric times by the Illyrians and their unknown predecessors, the island of Hvar became a Greek colony in the 4th c. B.C. Greeks from the Aegean island of Paros founded the town of Pharos near what today is Stari Grad and, on the site of the town of Hvar, an autonomous settlement (Dimos) which was subsequently united with Pharos. In the early 3rd c. B.C. following the reign of Dimitrije, a Greek from Hvar who married the Illyrian queen Triteuta and was a Roman ally for a time, the island was seized by the Romans. They pushed the local Illyrian inhabitants towards the east and the hilly parts of the island while retaining for themselves the fertile flat land and the foothills where they developed many small settlements. Most of the new Roman settlers lived on country estates.

During Roman rule life in the island declined in comparison with the Greek period, and the Roman Pharia, although evolving from the Greek Pharos, could not compare with its predecessor. Nor was the Roman settlement, which stood on the site of the town of Hvar, of any importance. It was situated at the eastern edge of what is now the main square (Dolac), then a small sea inlet, while Hvar's oldest prehistoric settlement stood on the slope below the present fortress.

The prehistoric period left Neolithic traces in caves and Illyrian *tumuli* from the Bronze and Iron Age. From Greek times date the remains of Pharos and the observation tower (Tor) above Jelsa, and from Roman times the poorly preserved remains of villas, some of which were provided with central heating installations.

Very little is known about the history of the island from the 3rd c. B.C. till the 12th c. apart from the highly important fact that in the 7th c. the island was settled by the Slavs to become soon completely slavicized both ethnographically and as regards place names which without exceptions are Croatian. For a long time the island was ruled by a Neretva tribe which controlled the Makarska coastal area and a group of large islands (Brač, Hvar, Vis, Korčula, Lastovo). At the end of the 11th c. the island came under the control of Hungarian-Croatian kings, to change subsequently its supreme authority several times — including two Venetian occupations (1135 and 1278) — before finally coming under the control of the Venetian Republic (1420—1797).

The earliest beginnings of the town of Hvar have to be sought in the distant past. It is not known precisely when the town developed into the leading insular urban centre during the Middle Ages. Like other political communities of that period, the Neretva region, as a tribal product of the early Middle Ages, contained no towns, while the town of Hvar did not come into being during ancient times. It is therefore believed that the foundation of a bishopric in Stari Grad in 1147 which developed into modern Hvar at the end of the 12th c.

or in the 13th c., led to the development of urban life. This would conform to the typical development pattern of most European towns.

The beginning of Venetian rule in 1278 (the second Venetian occupation) meant much more in the life of the island than a mere change of supreme authority and secession from the Hungarian-Croatian state. For it altered completely the role of the town in relation to the island as a whole. While until then the town of Hvar was autonomous in the area which was under the rule of a *župan* — who was either appointed by the supreme ruler or confirmed by him from among the old nobility, — with the arrival of the new, Venetian rule the town council gained control of the island and the feudal system disappeared together with the institution of the *župan*. One part of the old tribal or feudal nobility accepted the new order and joined the city council — now called the Great Council — but were compelled to live in the town together with those very city elders who had brought about the respective political change. Thus came into being the youngest commune in Dalmatia. Soon after the town had been given control of the island, Venice demanded and assisted in the construction of city walls, a fortress, a bishop's palace, a government palace, an arsenal, — everything that was required for the creation of an urban environment.

Subsequent developments did not alter the situation. With the arrival of Napoleon's administration in 1806, the area of the commune — together with the island of Vis — became an administrative district with the seat in Hvar.

After the Venetian occupation, a tribal noble, Galeša Slavogosti, tried in 1310 to free the island from Venetian rule, but his attempt failed. The event marked the beginning of the decline of the prestige of both the feudal and the urban nobility, while the following century brought the first beginnings of emancipation from the exclusive control of the aristocratic Great Council. In the early 15th c. the free Hvar spirit — developed in the continual struggle with the sea and in the permanent contact with foreign countries through Hvar Port — became increasingly manifest within the framework of local brotherhoods, which embraced the entire population and, in the conditions of the time, acted as actual local assemblies. As early as in the mid-15th c. the village of Vrbanj achieved a notable victory: the right to elect a parson which previously was the exclusive privilege of the Chapter of Hvar. This novelty marked the beginning of political consciousness among the rural population, and this was a necessary pre-condition for the development of political life among the peasants.

This helps to explain the emergence of Matija Ivanić, a shipowner from Vrbanj and Vrboska, who electrified the already restless popular masses and started a rebellion demanding the equality of the commoners with the nobility. While still a young man (in 1487) Ivanić, together with a group of Vrbanj shippers, erected the chapel of St. Nicholas, the patron of seamen, on the island's highest point (626 m) in demonstration of the unity of spirit and the sea orientation of the Hvar people. By 1510 the movement had gathered momentum, to continue, with varying intensity, till 1610 when an agreement was signed under which commoners and nobles were proclaimed politically equal classes. The agreement may be regarded as a great victory of the people. The spiritual victory becomes even clearer in the light of the fact that from the 16th c. onwards there were no patricians or any traces of their influence left in the island's central villages.

The signing of the agreement introduced a new spirit, and the solidarity of the citizens became manifest in common cultural aspirations. Even the counting of time in Hvar became based on the year of the signing of the peace: the rear door of the Arsenal carries the inscription *anno pacis I* (1611), and the entrance door of the Theatre *anno secundo pacis* (1612).

Hvar suffered very cruel attacks from the Venetian fleet at the time of the rebellion in the early 16th c. and two Turkish onslaughts (1539 and 1571) which led to consequences that are still remembered (the fire of Vrboska, the destruction by fire of the old communal archives, the destruction of public buildings and churches in Hvar, the siege of the Jelsa fortress described in a poem by A. K. Miošić).

Venice ruled Hvar (after the attempts in 1135 and 1278) without a break from 1420 till 1797. Venetian rule was followed by the Austrian occupation (till 1806) and the French occupation (till 13 November, 1813), and finally the second Austrian occupation which ended with the First World War when Hvar became part of the newly created Yugoslavia.

The town of Hvar flourished and reached its greatest architectural boom in the 15th and 16th centuries — the period which gave it its present stylistic characteristics. In the 16th and early 17th c. the town of Hvar shone brightly on the Croatian cultural horizon. However, the 17th c., a century of wars, slowed down Hvar's powerful cultural development. The subsequent centuries brought a stagnation in Hvar life which became intensified under the decadent Venetian rule and especially later on, in the mid-19th c., when as a result of the arrival of the steamship the function of the town's protective harbour (so important to sailing ships) lost much of its importance. This brought to an end the old development cycle of the town. It required the arrival of modern means of transport and the revival of agriculture to open new prospects which were to give the island the characteristics of an expressly tourist region with agriculture seeking to adjust itself to the new economy. After the Second World War and all the sufferings it brought, a truly new era opened in the island. It was a period of great enthusiasm and vigorous activity. And just as they played an important role in the country's national liberation struggle, in which many distinguished themselves as outstanding fighters and efficient organizers (Hvar military bases, hospitals and military camps are all well known), the Hvar people now found in the newly liberated country real support for their needs.

As at the time of the old statute, the town of Hvar today is the administrative seat of the commune. The historical difference lies in the fact that the modern commune is based on the socialist principles of the Yugoslav self-management system.

THE NAME OF THE ISLAND AND THE IMPORTANCE OF HVAR PORT

It is generally accepted that the name Hvar derives from the name Pharos which was given by Greeks from the Aegean island of Paros to their new settlement of the site of present-day Stari Grad as far back as the 4th c. B. C.

There also exists a so-called Italian name for the island (Lesina) which is of comparatively recent date (18th c.) and a variation of the names Lesna, Lisna or Liesna which appear in all texts from earlier centuries and suggest the Slavonic origin of the word. The word *lesna, lisna* or *liesna* derives from the verb *lijezati* which means to enter (i. e. to dock), and the name derived from it came into use at the time when people from the Neretva area, referring to the port of Hvar, would say that they were going to enter the port or *ljesna, lesna* or *lisna*. The seamen of the past and those who knew only the harbour of Hvar extended the name to the whole of the island. Later on, both for the island and the port of Hvar there prevailed the use of the name which came into existence in Stari Grad in old-Greek times, or perhaps earlier, and was subsequently extended to the other, nautically more important settlement and its harbour. Thus came into being Novi Hvar (New Hvar — Neos Pharos) while Old Pharos became Stari (= old) Hvar. Crystallization of the names led to the acceptance of the name Stari Grad for the oldest settlement, and Hvar for the port and the seat of the mediaeval and the later modern commune.

CULTURAL DEVELOPMENT OF THE TOWN OF HVAR

Cultural life was probably already flourishing in the town of Hvar at the time when the town began to develop, especially after it became the seat of the Hvar commune (1278), the youngest autonomous commune in Dalmatia, and was chiefly due to material prosperity and intellectual achievements.

Religious plays were probably performed in front of the Cathedral as early as in the 14th c. Intensive theatrical activity was a natural correlative of the free and progressive man as also was an abundant literature. Patricians and commoners alike used to send their sons to study in Italy, but even without this, a humanistic outlook pervaded Hvar life. This is why

Hvar — The old town walls (14th c.) and the Pakleni Islands

Hvar — View from Fort Napoleon (241 m)

Hvar

Hvar — The unfinished Gothic Hektorović House above the city gate (15th c.)

20

Hvar — View from the Castle
(fortica)

Hvar — Main street with well from
1475

Hvar — The Cathedral and the renaissance bell tower

Painting of the Madonna from the Hektorović altar in the Cathedral (13th c.)

Cathedral — Interior

23

Hvar — View from the air

Cliffs, pine-trees and the sea

Hvar

The interior of the Hvar Theatre

Hvar — Arsenal

»The Last Supper« in the
Franciscan monastery in Hvar

The Franciscan monastery in
Hvar

The cloister of the Franciscan monastery in
Hvar (15th c.)

The jube in the Franciscan church in Hvar with paintings by Martin Benetović (above) and Francesco da Santacroce (below)

Hvar — The municipal beach

Hvar — The renaissance Loggia with Hotel »Palace«

The old quayside known as Fabrika (16th c.)

Hotel »Delfin« with the renaissance chapel of St. George on the old quayside (Fabrika)

Hotel »Amfora«

Hotel »Amfora« — The interior

the 16th century could produce a Vičenco Priboević who, speaking in St. Mark's Church in 1525, first described the essential characteristics of the town and its importance, to devote the rest of his speech to the greatness of Slavdom.

The humanistic culture of Petar Hektorović, the builder of Tvrdalj in Stari Grad (1487—1572), did not become manifest in any imitation of old values, but brought into being the first Croatian realistic epos *Ribanje i ribarsko prigovaranje* (Fishing and Fishermen's Conversations) in which the poet described local life and the figure of the local fisherman, expressed natural and direct inter-human relations, and proved his national consciousness.

Hanibal Lucić (1485—1553) too brought fame to his island with his play *Robinja* (The Woman Slave), the first temporal drama in Yugoslav literature, and a collection of love poems *(Pisni ljuvene)*. Both poets write in sure, firm and beautiful Croatian and develop their themes with a healthy realism.

In this activity and as regards quality there is no difference between patricians and commoners: inspired by the same humanism, they create valuable literary works, as for instance Martin Benetović, a man of universal talents, who wrote The Woman of Hvar *(Hvarkinja)* and The Comedy of Raskot (Komedija od Raskota) while at the same time giving musical instruction and painting pictures for the Franciscan Monastery. All these men are not only the protagonists and the expression of the local culture but also co-founders of Croatian literature. It should be noted that the Hvar literary circle developed its liveliest activity in the 16th century. Not even Turkish pressure, which was directly felt on the island for 200 years and which reached its culmination in the 16th c. before the Battle of Lepanto

(1571), could disturb that rich literary production; in fact, it only encouraged it providing the authors with topical themes.

The completion of the theatre in Hvar in 1612 was a kind of cultural manifestation of all classes of the local population. Symbolizing the just acquired right of all classes to participate in the administration (1610) — a unique phenomenon in Europe, — the theatre was founded on a communal basis and entitles Hvar to boast that it possessed Europe's first communal theatre which from its very beginning was managed with equal care by both the people's assembly and the oligarchic council. Hvar thus was the first to prove that the purpose of a theatre is not to serve only a closed circle of nobility but the people as a whole.

In the 17th c. the patrician Marin Gazarović wrote in, and translated into, the national language, and the commoner Ivan Franjo Biundović wrote (in Italian) the first European fiction work and a history of England.

CULTURAL MONUMENTS OF THE TOWN OF HVAR

The town of Hvar is situated in the island's most accessible place on a wide bay which looks towards the south-west and is protected by a chain of small islands *(Pakleni otoci)*. Due to this favourable situation Hvar has always played an important role in Adriatic shipping and is still the busiest port of call of coastal shipping in the Adriatic islands.

The oldest settlements which once stood on the site of modern Hvar have left practically no visible traces. Both the Greek settlement Dimos and the subsequent Roman settlement were situated at the farthest end of the former sea inlet (now Dolac Square), extending beyond the present Cathedral on the eastern side of the square where a well-preserved section of a Roman cobbled road has been discovered at a depth of 2 metres. Many centuries later a Benedictine monastery was erected on this site, and in the 13th c. was converted into a bishop's palace — a function it still has today. The mediaeval town developed in the 12th and 13th c. on the northern side of the present square, below the former Illyrian fortress, and the southern part of the town began to rise on the remains of what probably was a fortification of Neretva Slavs during the first decades of the 15th c.

The town square

Covering an area of 4,500 sq. metres, it is the largest square in Dalmatia. Until the end of the 15th c. it was surrounded by gardens. The area in front of the City Loggia was covered with stone slabs in 1537; the existing pavement dates from 1780. In the centre of the square stands a well, erected in 1520 and reconstructed in 1780 and 1830. The crown of the well and the inscription date from 1830.

In front of the City Loggia stands a stone pedestal (*štandarac*) with a socket for the flagstaff. In the past it was the place where communal decisions were announced and delinquents exposed. The pedestal bears the inscription 1735 and the initials of the then reigning Count (the representative of the government) Vicenzo Gritti (VG).

The town walls

The part of Hvar which is called Grad and stands below the citadel is surrounded by Romanesque walls dating from the end of the 13th and the early 14th c. and is flanked by square, crennelated side towers with very attractive doors. The main gate of Grad leads to the lower part of the square; the eastern gate near the Cathedral is of a later date and bears the year of construction (1454).

Fortifications

The citadel on the top of the hill above the town was built in the mid-16th c. (1557) on the site of the old mediaeval castle. Its extremely graceful design includes certain elements from Napoleonic times. At the beginning of the 19th c. the Austrian military authorities added the barracks and the building for the main guard. The Pompeian red and yellow date from that time. The citadel is now a popular recreation centre which is especially attractive at night.

Slightly to the east, on the top of the steep hill of Sv. Nikola Viši (St. Nicholas the Higher) which dominates the citadel stands Fort Napoleon which was built by the French army in 1811 at the order od Marshal Marmont. The project was designed and its execution supervised by French army engineers Major Rubbi and Captain Tracy. The construction work was done by locally recruited labour under the supervision of local masters (Bertapelle from Vrboska). The fortress now houses an astronomical and seismographical observatory.

The 16th-century Greek-orthodox monastery of St. Veneranda which once stood above the main swimming beach was turned by the French into a small fortification (1807) which they named *Batterie de droite* and which became popularly known as Baterija. The French administration had the campanile of the monastery church pulled down and transferred to Sutivan in the island of Brač. It was one of the four Hvar bell towers which were regarded as the most beautiful specimens of their kind in Dalmatia. In 1953 the Baterija was reconstructed and arranged as an open-air theatre.

With the stones obtained by pulling down the Augustinian monastery and church of St. Nicholas the Lower (*Sv. Nikola Niži;* the site is now occupied by the cemetery) the French built another fortification (1811) which they called *Batterie de gauche,* — a small graceful structure which still stands on the left side of the harbour entrance on top of the promontory closing the port but which is hidden behind pine trees. After the withdrawal of the French the building was renamed after Andreas Hofer, the leader of the Tyrolean rebellion against Napoleon.

The Austrian fortification and barracks on the islet of Galešnik guarding the entrance to the harbour were built in 1832, and the quay in 1833.

Patrician Palaces

We shall mention only some of the best known. Above the city gate rises the unfinished Hektorović House with coats-of-arms cut in stone and with lovely windows in the florid Gothic style of the 15th c. The entrance into the house, first under the covered walk which links the house with the city wall and then along the inner staircase, is extremely original in concept. The first street to the right of the house and running parallel with the square leads to Lucić-Paladinić House which stands immediately behind the corner and leans against the city wall. It is an imposing building with two rows of Gothic windows, which can be seen from the garden on the southern side of the building, and a balcony with a beautiful stone balustrade. The window arches are more pointed and of simpler design which is an obvious sign that the building is older than Hektorović House. The coat-of-arms decorating the crown of the well which stands in a corner of the vestibule is identical with that above the street entrance: a lily and the black wing of the family Lucić, another ancient Hvar noble family. The building is called Lucić-Paladinić after a branch of the Lucić family which gained military fame in the first struggles with the Turks in the late 15th c. and adopted the same coat-of-arms as the family Lucić. The building was the first monumental house to be built in the town of Hvar.

East of this building and in the same street stands a house on the city walls which was the private property of the poet Petar Hektorović and, next to it, the house of the old noble family Slavogosti (Gazari). Behind these buildings, but no longer on the city walls, can be seen another two imposing structures which, although in a bad state of repair, are stylistically highly interesting. One is the remains of an early Gothic house which also belonged to the family Gazari and which dominates the area enclosed by four streets; the other is a block of houses of the patrician family Jakša which occupies a large site by the church of the Holy Spirit (Sv. Duh). The façade is decorated with the same coat-of-arms of pure renaissance concept and design as is that on Hektorović House, because the two families were of the same descent.

In Novak-Soletti house which stands between these two buildings can be seen a unique specimen of the coat-of-arms of the family Radašinić with the pretentious motif of a two-headed eagle. In the vicinity stands the town's oldest well from 1475 (MCDLXXV) decorated with the figure of the Venetian lion holding a closed book of St. Mark the Evangelist, — a sign that the well was erected in wartime.

On the other side of the square, in the suburban district known as Burg, there are two buildings worth seeing: one is Hvar's most beautiful palace which belonged to the commoner and later nobleman Vukašinović and is built in renaissance and baroque style with 7 balconies on the front side, a terrace, massive latticework on the groundfloor windows, and a monumental gate; the other is Kasandrić-Gargurić House which has attractive 15th-century Gothic windows, convoluted pillars and — as a contrast — a simple Gothic entrance door. Everywhere in the town and in the Burg district there are interesting architectural details, — corners, staircases and small terraces — in early Gothic, Gothic, renaissance or baroque style.

City Loggia and Clock Tower

Once they formed part of a group of government buildings (Count's Palace) which were pulled down at the turn of the century to make room for the present Hotel »Palace«. The present Loggia was built at the end of the 15th c., enlarged in the early 16th c., and reconstructed after the Turkish onslaught in 1571. The building bears the characteristics of the high renaissance and the building masters of that period. The decorative pyramids (giuglie) on the balustrade of the terrace are in baroque style. From 1868 the Loggia was used as a café till 1971 when it was reconstructed in neo-renaissance style and now serves as the banquet hall of Hotel Palace.

The Clock Tower stands in one of the towers of the former Count's Palace where it was erected in the second half of the 15th c. The present bell dates from 1564 and was repaired in the 18th and again in the 19th c. when a new clock was installed.

Of the former Count's Palace only the very massive crown of the well in the courtyard of Hotel »Palace«, the lintel of the chapel from 1612, and two Venetian lions from the façades of the demolished buildings have survived.

Arsenal, Granary and Old Port Installations

The construction of the Arsenal began in the 13th c. to provide a safe shelter for the Hvar war galleon which every commune was obliged to keep available for the state naval fleet. The building's present design dates from the 17th c. when the first floor with the theatre and a room for naval requirements were added. The only surviving remnant of the galleon is the figure-head (polena) which is kept in the theatre.

The Granary (fontik or fondaco = storehouse) on the north side of the Arsenal served as a communal storehouse for reserve food supplies. The building has large vaults and massive walls of dressed stone with the numbers of the individual entrances cut in stone. It now houses a self-service shop.

Below the square and in front of the Loggia stands an enclosed anchorage for small craft known as mandrač (from Greek mandra = stable). The mandrač was first mentioned in 1459. Its present balustrade with baroque pyramids and an inscription on its eastern section was erected in 1795 by Marco Dandolo, the penultimate Count (Venice's representative).

The massive stone quay extending left from the mandrač in front of the Arsenal and to the right (westwards) to the small wood by the swimming beach dates from the mid-16th c. (1554) and is one of the oldest in Europe. Built at the same time as the big Hvar citadel and known as Fabrika it testifies to the important role played by Hvar in merchant and naval shipping of the time.

Churches and Bell Towers

One of the most impressive sights of Hvar, and especially of its main square, is the Cathedral with the renaissance bell tower which were built by masters Nikola Karlić and Marko Milić Pavlović in the 16th c. The bell tower of the Cathedral and those of the other Hvar churches (St. Mark's, Franciscan, and St. Veneranda's /demolished/) are regarded by experts as the most beautiful in Dalmatia. They are built in renaissance style, but like all provincial bell towers they contain traces of earlier styles.

The reconstructed Cathedral was once the church of a Benedictine monastery. The present structure dates from the 16th—17th c. but still includes architectural elements and stone furnishings from the older churches standing on that site. It is not known how the church, which was originally dedicated to St. Mary, came to obtain its present patron (St. Stephen). Judging by the façade, the building belongs to the group of churches with a trilobate gable. Some of the decorations and the windows contain traces of Gothic influence, and the portal and the main altar are of a similar design. This type of portal is believed to have been introduced in Dalmatia by Petar Andrijić of Korčula, the builder of the Church of the Saviour in Dubrovnik.

The central section of the building belonged to the former church and includes one of the most beautiful choirs to be built in Dalmatia in the 15th c. The choir was reconstructed by Mark Anthony the Venetian in the 16th c. The year 1573 carved in the stone indicates the time of the reconstruction. At the entrance to the

41

choir stand two Romanesque pulpits from the original church, with altars and two massive lecterns below them. On the steps leading to the choir, the Croatian grave inscription of Niko Vukašinović from 1607.

Also from the older church are the 15th-century stone reliefs Madonna with the Saints and The Flagellation, a variant of the work of Juraj Dalmatinac in Split Cathedral. The new part of the three-aisled church contains nine baroque marble altars of identical design. All date from the 17th c. and were donated by guilds, through endowments or by patrician families. Different in style is the chapel and altar of St. Prosperius north of the central chapel.

The following is a brief description of the altar pieces as seen when walking round the church from right to left starting from the main entrance. St. Lucy on the first altar to the right is the work of an unknown Venetian painter; Domenico Umberti's Madonna with St. Joseph on the second altar was acquired in 1692. (On the floor between the two altars, the gravestone of the noblewoman Lukrecija Fasaneo of 1670 which was brought here from St. Joseph's chapel on the water front /Fabrika/). In front of the third altar, the grave of Bishop Priuli of 1692, and on the altar the painting Madonna with the Donator which is believed to be the work of Stefano Celesti from the mid-17th c. The Madonna on the next altar, which was erected by the Hektorović family (see inscription in front of the altar below the wooden floor) is one of the oldest in Dalmatia (about 1220). The painting is a work of the proto-Venetian school which developed from the original mosaic workshops in Venice. The Chapel of the Holy Cross with the yellow and black marble floor contains no paintings. Next comes the main altar with the painting The Madonna and St. Stephen (the church's patron) by

Palma Junior (Jacopo Negretti, 1544—1628). North of the main chapel, the chapel with the altar of Bishop Andreis from 1678, the sarcophagus of St. Prosperius from 1859 (A. Braselin da Padova), and the gravestone of Bishop Duboković Nadalini from 1874, — but also without an altar piece. The baroque altars along the north wall of the church are as follows: the altar of the Holy Sacrament with bishop's graves without inscriptions and, next to it, the altar with a painting of the Madonna and St. Anthony (from 1678), probably by Stefano Celesti; next comes the altar with a small 15th-century Pietà by the Spanish artist Juan Boschettus (within a larger painting by A. Gradinelli from 1728), and finally the last altar on the north side of the church next to the portal with the painting of St. Petrus by an unidentified Venetian painter but bearing the signature of its restorer, Renis of Brindisi (1804). The treasures of the sacristy are on display in the Cathedral's collection at the Bishop's Palace. A small guidebook of the collection is available.

The Church of the Holy Spirit (Sv. Duh) in the town (Grad). Built in the 15th c. it has an interesting broken arch above the portal and a Romanesque figure of a saint in the space for the lunette. The rose window is placed outside the axis of the building. Inside the church an altar piece by Alessandro Varotari of Padua (1580—1650) and a small 15th-century painting The Descent of the Holy Spirit by the same Spanish painter (Boschettus) who painted the Pietà in the Cathedral (the painting is temporarily loaned to the Cathedral collection).

Benedictine Church and Convent. Founded during the reign of Bishop Milani (1644—1667) and situated in the house of Hanibal Lucić which was bequeathed for the purpose by Julija Gazzari, the wife of his son Antun. The baroque chapel with heraldic motives of the family Lucić on the façade contains a painting by Liberale Cozzo from 1750.

SS. Cosmas and Damian. The only Romanesque building in Hvar (apart from the town walls), with baroque alterations dating from a later period. The church stands between the Clock Tower, Hotel »Palace« and Hektorović House on the town walls.

Former Dominican Church of St. Mark. Now in ruins with only the outer shell and bell tower surviving.

The apse of the church now contains an archaeological collection, and the shell of the former church with the collection of fragments of stone architecture is used for vocal and chamber music concerts. The bell tower houses the grave of the Croatian musician Josip Rafaelli (1767—1843).

Next to St. Mark's is the former **chapel of St. Roch** (now an appartment) from the 15th c. with a highly interesting rustic façade.

At the farther end of the old Venetian Quayside stands the renaissance chapel of St. Joseph »na Fabrici« with a semicircular gable. The chapel houses a painting with a panoramic view of Hvar.

The small chapel above the town known as **Kruvenica** (from the old-Slavonic word *horugva* = flag) dates from the 16th c. It contains an inscription from 1550. The chapel was under the patronage of the Count (the representative of the Venetian state) and the commander of the fortress.

The Church of the Annunciation. A 14th-century building situated in the Burg district. On the main altar of the church a 16th-century painting of Our Lady. On the right-hand altar St. Barbara (Venetian school, 18th c.) and lovely ceremonial candelabra from the 18th c. The altar piece on the left-hand altar is a work of T. Kukolja, a baroque painter from Boka kotorska. The lunette of the renaissance façade contains a relief of the Annunciation executed in the manner of Niccolo Fiorentino.

CULTURAL INSTITUTIONS

The town's historical archives, founded in 1950 and known as the Centre for the Protection of Cultural Heritage (*Centar za zaštitu kulturne baštine*), are kept at Hanibal Lucić's villa.

The Arsenal houses the **Gallery of Modern Painting** and the **Hvar Theatre.** Founded in 1612, the Theatre is one of the oldest and the first communal theatre in Europe. The present furnishings date from 1803.

The Cathedral Collection in the Bishop's residence contains church vestments, lace and vessels from various periods, a highly valuable crosier of Bishop Pritić from the 16th c. (a work of the domestic goldsmith Pavao Dubravčić), a collection of mitres, parchment manuscripts, etc.

The Bishop's Palace was formerly a Benedictine monastery. The old inscriptions in the building (the oldest dates from 1249) mostly record past reconstructions of the building, the latest of which was carried out in the 1870s. The tasteful furnishings of the rooms date partly from the 18th c. and partly from the time after the last reconstruction (about 1870).

The Library of the Chapter, the largest library in the island, was founded by Bishop Tomasini in 1461. It is kept in a separate room above the sacristy which also houses the Chapter's archives.

The Open-air Theatre (*Ljetna pozornica*) was set up in 1953 within the old French fortification on the site of the former Greek Orthodox monastery of St. Veneranda.

In front of the theatre, a small circular Austrian powder magazine (known as *Mlin*) with a two-headed stone eagle dating from 1822, and nearby the **Meteorological Station** founded in 1858 by the natural scientist Dr Grgur Bučić.

The Astronomical Observatory is in Fort Napoleon. A massive stone cross (*Kamen križ*) dating from the 16th c. stands on a cliff above the town from where one can obtain a beautiful view of the main square and a panorama of the lay-out of the town.

Franciscan monastery. Built in 1461 on a site known as *Sridnji rat* by the old field chapel of the Holy Cross. The monastery's renaissance cloister was built at the same time as the church (between 1465 and 1471). The year MCCCCLXXXVIIII (1489) carved at the bottom of the roof arch outside the entrance into the cloister may indicate the year of the completion of the building. The portal with the lunette which contains a relief depicting the Madonna with Jesus was executed by master Niccolo Fiorentino (who was under the influence of the great Donatello and died in 1505). The relief came into being between 1465 and 1470.

Originally, the church had only one chapel by the main aisle. The other two were built later on by Petar Andrijić, the builder of the Divona and the churches of the Saviour and the Annunciation in Dubrovnik.

The bell tower is the oldest of Hvar's four bell towers, three of which still survive and are regarded as the most beautiful specimens of their kind in Dalmatia. They were built by masters Blaž Andrijević and Frano

Nikola Španić of Korčula. The wall surrounding the monastery dates from 1545, and the small baroque chapels lining the old approach to the monastery from the town (their continuity was broken before the war when the area was cut up into building lots) were erected by Marin Capello, the commander of the Adriatic fleet, in 1720.

The monastery was damaged by the Turks (led by ill-famed Uluč Alija) on the eve of the Battle of Lepanto (1571) but was soon reconstructed (1574). The graves now in the two northern chapels stood outside the church before the erection of the chapels. Together with the graves in the choir and in other parts of the church they belong to the families who founded the monastery. In front of the main altar the grave of Hanibal Lucić, the author of the Woman Slave (Robinja) and the Love Poems (Pisni ljuvene) with the initials A. L. (Annibal Lucić).

The main aisle of the church is divided into two sections by a monumental jube or chancel screen, which resembles an iconostasis. The wooden choir in high-renaissance style is the work of masters Franjo Čiočić of Korčula and Antun Špija of Zadar (1583).

The paintings on the main altar and on the two altars leaning against the western side of the chancel screen are the works of the Venetian painter Francesco de Santacroce (1516—1584) and are executed in the form of polyptychs (1583).

The iconostasis on the same (western) side surmounting the two altars and the door leading between them to the choir is decorated with six scenes from Christ's Passion by the local comediographer (the author of Hvarkinja and Komedija od Raskota) and organist Martin Benetović († 1607).

The monumental door leading between the two altars from the main aisle to the choir was commissioned by the Hvar patrician Frano Antun Bertučević.

The main aisle contains the altar piece »St. Francis receives the Stigmata« by Palma jun. who also painted the altar piece with St. Stephen on the main altar of the Cathedral. Palma was the artist in greatest demand in Dalmatia at the end of the 16th c.

On the altar in the north-eastern chapel, with the stone partition by Petar Andrijić, a crucifix by Leandro Bassano (1560—1623). The chapel clearly shows traces of Turkish devastation.

The church contains several interesting inscriptions: one, from 1574, refers to the reconstruction of the church, and one, from 1612, can be seen on the gravestone of Marija, the wife of the proveditor Pietro Semitecolo, whose efforts led to the peace settlement between the nobility and the common people in that year. Here too an inscription refers to »the second year of the peace« (ANNO SECUNDO PACIS) as does that on the door of the Theatre.

Above the inscription, a large wooden crucifix which formerly stood above the jube.

A side door leads to the cloister with a massive well (capacity 300 tons) in the centre. An old water duct, once used for the supply of ships and the local population, can be seen on the garden wall in front of the church under pine trees. The inscription on the well is damaged and hardly readable. It shows that the well was built by Rado of Šibenik in 14.. (15th c.).

A door on the southern side of the cloister leads into the monastery, and a second door to the old monastery refectory (now a museum) and the garden.

Vela Garška Cove near the town of Hvar

Vira Cove — ferry-boat terminal of the town of Hvar

The fish pond in Tvrdalj, the palace of the poet Petar Hektorović in Stari Grad (16th c.)

Jacopo Tintoretto: »Christ's Burial«
— in the Dominican Church in
Stari Grad

The Dominican Church in Stari
Grad

View of Stari Grad

Hotel »Helios« in Stari Grad

A section of the
Nautical Collection
in Stari Grad

Ferry-boat terminal
in Stari Grad

The village of Grablje

Lavender bushes on the island of Hvar

Sveta Nedjelja

The Ivanić-Boglić-Božić summer residence (15th—18th c.) in Milna

The fortified church of St. Mary (17th c.) in Vrboska

Vrboska

Antonio Sciuri: The Birth of St. Mary — Vrboska (17th c.)

Dol sv. Marije

Vrbanj — The church

Jelsa

Jelsa — View towards the sea

Jelsa — Sv. Ivan Square with
St. John's Chapel

Drawing-room in
Duboković-Nadalini House
in Jelsa

Jelsa — Hotel »Mina«

Jelsa — The cemetery chapel

61

Zastražišće

Gdinj — The old church of St. George (16th—17th c.)

Bogomolje — Monument to Fallen Fighters by Joko Knežević

Sućuraj

The Pakleni Islands off Hvar

The entire area of the western wall of the refectory is covered by a monumental painting (2.50 x 8 m) depicting the Last Supper which has brought Hvar worldwide fame. The clever use of perspective in the painting adds to the depth of the large hall. Modern experts attribute the work to Matteo Ingola, a painter from Ravenna (1585—1631). However, comparative methods indicate that it was probably painted by Palma jun. or by an artist from his close circle with his co-operation. According to a traditional belief surviving at the monastery the painting is a work of Matteo Rosselli. However, the stylistic and architectural motifs marking the painting exclude this possibility because Rosselli was a Florentine.

According to modern experts the painting came into being at the turn of the 16th and 17th c. and in a certain measure contains both Veronese's colours and Tintoretto's illumination and also the entire inventory of expression of the late-Venetian painting school of the 16th c.

The monastery houses many other interesting paintings including an Ecce Homo (17th c.), The Betrothal of St. Catharine (15th c., a painting from the workshop of Blaž Jurjev of Trogir), The Descent from the Cross (16th c.), Christ's Head (16th c.), St. Vincent of Ferrero (18th c., by G. B. Tiepolo), St. Peter of Alcantara (18th c.), a Madonna (17th c.), and some beautiful old wood carvings: The Annunciation (17th c.), St. John (16th c.), and St. Hieronymus (bas relief).

The Franciscan collection further contains several bibliographic rarities including a breviary from the 15th c., a copy of the Koran from the 17th c., and an atlas of Ptolemy printed in 1524 (Bilibaldo Pirkeymhera interprete, Noribergae), illuminated antiphonaries from the 15th c. (by fra Bone Razmilović), beautiful church vestments from the 14th c. and from the baroque period, old lace, a collection of old coins current in Hvar in the past, etc., etc.

The monastery's large book collection, started at the time of the foundation of the monastery, contains 53 incunabula (printed before the end of the 15th c.). The archives of the monastery are kept in a separate room. In the grounds of the monastery there is a small garden reserved for rest containing a huge cypress tree (200 years old) and wood carvings by fra Kazimir Bučić.

THE SURROUNDINGS OF THE TOWN OF HVAR

Pakleni islands (Pakleni otoci)

The name of this group of islets which protect the Hvar harbour and channel derives from the word *paklina* meaning pine resin which was used for coating wooden ships, especially Venetian warships, in the coves of the islets (Italian for 'to coat' is *spalmare*, hence the name of Palmižana Cove).

On St. Clement island (Sveti Kliment), or the Large Island (Veliki otok) as it was still called in the 15th c., stands a 14th-century chapel dedicated to the same saint. The inscriptions in the chapel referring to the Battle of Lissa (1866) add to the historical value of this monument. The island was inhabited by the Illyrians (Illyrian tumuli from the first millennium B. C.) and the Romans (remains of the Roman settlement Solina).

The islet of Jerolim (originally called Rasohatac) derives its present name from Jerolim Grivičić, a local nobleman and Franciscan monk, who was presented with the islet by the Hvar Commune in 1497. Grivičić is believed to have commissioned the paintings of Francesco Santacroce in the monastery church and built a small hospice on the islet the ruins of which still survive.

From the town of Hvar towards Pelegrin Promontory

From the citadel (mid-15th c.) to the Vira ferry-boat terminal in the north, the Austrian watch-tower (Smokovnik, 1839) on the ridge of the peninsula, and through a lovely wood to the comparatively bare **Pelegrin Promontory** with the lighthouse. The area includes the prehistoric cave known as **Markova špilja** with highly valuable archaeological findings (still under investigation by Prof. Dr Grga Novak, President of the Yugoslav Academy). A small tunnel on the southern side of the promontory leads to Hotel »Sirena« and the coves Mala Garška and Vela Garška (Little Greece, Big Greece).

PLACES IN THE ISLAND OF HVAR

The island of Hvar is marked by great variety. Natural attractions and numerous cultural and historical monuments can be found everywhere and the island's places and villages provide attractive excursion spots.

Hvar — Brusje — Grablje — Selca — Stari Grad by road

The first village to be reached behind Hvar on the road to Stari Grad is **Brusje** (6.5 km from Hvar). The village developed from temporary dwellings of shepherds in the early 16th c. The church (from 1731) has been enlarged on two occasions. On the façade, the figure of St. George on horseback. The altar piece in the church depicting St. Anthony the Abbot and other saints by B. Zelotti (1532—1592) was brought here from the Dominican monastery in Hvar.

The figure of St. George in the altar piece decorating the main altar is set against a background showing the islands of Brač and Šolta (Split Channel). The painting is a gift of the contemporary Croatian painter Ivo Dulčić of Brusje. The Rectory was originally the country seat of Bishop Bonajuti (1736—1759). The elevation with these buildings and the local cemetery commands a wide panoramic view.

On the right-hand side of the road before Brusje, and on the left behind Brusje, on the road to Stari Grad, stand the ruins of two small patrician summer residences from the 16th c. The first is called Njivice, the second Moncirovo (*maceria* = ruins).

Five kilometres behind Brusje we reach the village of **Velo Grablje** which came into existence before the 15th c. developing probably from the country estates of the old patrician families Ozor and Gazari.

A lovely walk along the bed of a dried-up brook will bring us from Velo Grablje to **Malo Grablje** 2 km below. Clinging precariously to the steep rock side, the village looks like a pirates' stronghold. It is no longer inhabited, the inhabitants having moved down into new houses in Milna Cove. From Malo Grablje one can proceed to Milna returning from there to Hvar either by the ancient road or by ship.

Continuing on the road from Velo Grablje towards Stari Grad we reach the watershed near Ozrin (altitude 300 m) and from there descend to the small village of **Selca.** Selca is a good starting point for pleasant excursions to Gomilica, to the island's highest point (Sv. Niko,

626 m), etc. Behind Selca the road winds down for several kilometres before reaching the valley and entering Stari Grad (at Ploče).

From Hvar to Stari Grad by sea

By ordinary motor-boat the distance (22 km) can be covered within 3 hours.

After leaving the town harbour we sail along the southern shore of the island towards Cape Pelegrin, the island's westernmost point, and along the channel between Hvar and the islet of St. Clement and past the coves of Vela Grčka and Mala Grčka which offered safe shelter to shipping in the Middle Ages.

Of the many attractive coves and inlets along the coast one should mention Parja Cove with a prehistoric site **(Markova špilja)** on the hillside and, further east, Duga luka. In between lies the islet of Duga. Further east is Sokolica Cove and behind it Vela Vira with the remains of a bishop's summer residence from the 16th c. and the ruins of two chapels. In Mala Vira, the remains of a Roman villa and a Franciscan summer residence. On the slopes, a number of prehistoric tumuli (Illyrian graves). The concentric arrangement of the tumuli had ritual significance: the spirits of ancestors defend and protect (a custom already referred to by Homer).

Beyond Vira is Jagodna, the island's most thickly wooded cove. To the east lies Kosmača promontory with a lovely pine wood. In the **Carnica** area an interesting subterranean cave.

At Lozna, an inscription from the 18th c. records a large catch of fish. Stinica is the harbour of the village of Brusje and has a stone jetty. At the entrance to Tatinja an imposing cliff and, further on, the rocky slopes of Grabovac. At Lučišće the remains of the villa of the patrician family Bartučević and a well preserved chapel. The Bartučević family gave the 16th-century humanists and poets Jerolim and Hortenzije (his son). On the hill of Gračišće stood a prehistoric fortification. On Lompić promontory which protects Gračišće Cove, the remains of a prehistoric fortification from the 2nd millennium B.C. Pottery from the Illyrian and Graeco-Roman periods were found here. The fortification guarded the approach to the Bay of Stari Grad. Behind Gračišće, the coves Račindol, Konopljikova and Maslinica (with summer houses of Hvar patricians and sea captains' families).

On the opposite side of the bay, at Kabal which protects the Bay of Stari Grad, are the two coves (Tiha and Zavala) mentioned by Hektorović in his famous work »Fishing and Fishermen's Conversations«.

Towards the southern side of the island

Milna — 6 km from the town of Hvar, can be reached by the old road, or by motor-boat (25 minutes). The place is situated on a lovely bay with four large beaches, one of which can be approached only from the sea. On the eastern slopes above the bay, the village of Malo Grablje.

Further west on the bay the baroque summer residence of the Ivanić family (descendants of Matija Ivanić), now in the possession of the Boglić-Božić family. Built in the 17th c. on the foundations of an older structure from the 15th c. it is the most beautiful summer residence an the island. It now houses an inn. The building has a fortified courtyard with loopholes, iron-studded doors, farm buildings of baroque design, and a number of interesting stylistic details. On the staircase in the house the coat-of-arms of the Ivanić family. The mural drawings date from the second half of the 19th c., and the two realistic stone busts of members of the family from the 17th c.

Zaraće — 40 minutes by motor-boat (about 7 km from the town of Hvar). Situated on a mild slope between Milna and Dubovica, this small village is now becoming deserted. The local church, dedicated to Our Lady, was developed from an earlier structure built about 1530.

Dubovica — 50 minutes from Hvar by motor-boat. Above the beautiful beach, the summer residence of the family Kasandrić from the 18th/19th c., — now an inn.

Sveta Nedjelja — 1 hour by motor-boat from Hvar. Situated on a rocky elevation dominated by the island's highest point (Sv. Nikola, 626 m) below a cave with remains of an Augustinian monastery which stood here from the 15th c. till 1787. The village is approached from the beach along a winding path which runs through a small pine wood. Sveta Nedjelja is a famous centre for the production of the best types of Hvar red wine *(plavac)*.

Before the present century when they obtained their present church the villagers used to worship in the old monastery church in the cave. On the main altar in the new church, the altar piece St. Hieronymus and the Saints (by Baldissero d'Anna); on the side altar, a smaller painting (Our Lady of Cintura) by an unidentified master from the first half of the 18th c. The church also contains a painting of the Crucifixion by Juraj Plančić (1899—1930) of Stari Grad.

Zavala — about 80 m above the sea, two hours by motor-boat from Hvar. The village has a harbour with a jetty and — through Yugoslavia's longest road tunnel (1,400 m) — a road link with Jelsa. Zavala is famous for its

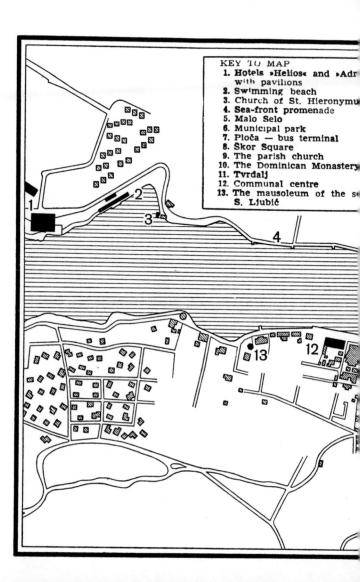

KEY TO MAP
1. Hotels »Helios« and »Adr
with pavilions
2. Swimming beach
3. Church of St. Hieronymu
4. Sea-front promenade
5. Malo Selo
6. Municipal park
7. Ploča — bus terminal
8. Skor Square
9. The parish church
10. The Dominican Monastery
11. Tvrdalj
12. Communal centre
13. The mausoleum of the s
S. Ljubić

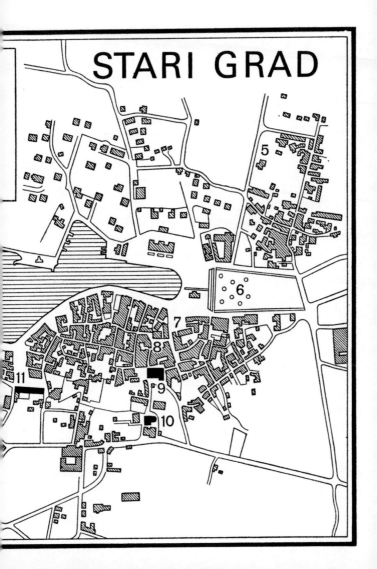

STARI GRAD

excellent white wine *(bogdanjuša)*. Below the village, a string of beautiful beaches lapped by a crystal clear sea. The most attractive is at Petraščica (with a cave). The beaches gave the village its original name Zaca (from *žalca* which means beaches) by which the village harbour is still called.

Zavala's attractions include the summer residence of the family Duboković-Nadalini (Biedermeyer style, about 1830) with the chapel of St. George (1866); further west, the former residence of the first owner of Zavala, Count Tadije Kačić (about 1630), and the residence of Zavala's 18th-century owner with the old chapel of St. Peter (1727) at the eastern end of the village.

Šćedro — an islet 2,700 m off the coast, has a total area of 900 hectares and two well sheltered harbours which played an important role in Adriatic shipping history due to their protective qualities (*štedri* in old Slavonic means charitable; hence the name Šćedro). The islet offers pleasant walks, good swimming and beautiful views, especially on its western side (lovely view of Hvar's high mountain ridge especially at sunset). Šćedro's highest point is 110 m above sea level. The climate is milder than in Hvar and, due to night dew, grain crops used to be grown here in old times (see a plough from Šćedro in the Ethnographical Museum in Stari Grad).

The islet's historical monuments include well preserved Illyrian tumuli of imposing dimensions (known as *Kadunje gomile* because of the large number of a kind of snail called *kadunjaci* found on them) and the remains of a Dominican monastery and church of St. Mary of Charity (from the island's name) from 1465.

The small village of **Gromindolac** east of Zavala also has very attractive beaches. In the centre of the village stands Obradić-Machiedo House built in the 17th c. as one of the island's strongholds against pirates. Further east is Budić House, a lovely renaissance country estate by the sea built in the 16th c. for the family Lupi. It now belongs to the family Radonić of Pitve. In design and execution the building closely resembles Hanibal Lucić's villa in Hvar. Because of the threat of pirate attack the size of the windows was reduced in the 17th c.

STARI GRAD

The town is situated at the head of a long inlet (6 km) on the site of the old Greek Pharos and the later Roman Pharia. The Greek town covered an area of 1.28 hectares, i. e. a much smaller site than that of modern Stari Grad.

An 11-metre section of the original Greek town walls can still be seen in Tadić Gramotorov House. Built of massive stone blocks by the dry-stone technique (see the analogous structure of Tor above Jelsa) it formed part of the northern perimetrical town wall. A section of the eastern wall can be seen in the garden and part of Gramotorov House behind St. John's church (Sveti Ivan).

Stone blocks recovered from the ancient town walls were built into the foundations of the bell tower of the local parish church in the 18th c. An inscription in the bell tower says that the entrance into the Greek town from the sea was exactly on this spot (... DEDE-RUNT HUIUS PRIMORDIA MOLIS DE MOENIBUS URBIS RELIQUIAE ET QUA DEDERAT GRESSUM IN URBEM JANUA ...). In one of the gardens, in the centre of the area once covered by the old town, there stands an old well which is locally called the Greek Well.

Roman remains can be seen primarily in front of the parish church. A Roman public bath stood once on the site of the church of St. Roch, as indicated by an inscription on the church stairs.

The old-Christian baptismal immersion font, a deep basin (115 cm) in the shape of the cross dating from the 6th/7th c. was discovered in 1957 but is now covered in for safety reasons. It stands by the church of St. John (Sv. Ivan), formerly St. Mary's, originally the seat of a bishop. The church is the island's oldest Christian sacral centre (recorded in documents from 1332). The present appearance is partly Gothic, while the ground plan and the apse are Romanesque in style. The building was erected on the site of an ancient temple.

Of the palace of the poet Lucić only some sections of the inner courtyard have survived.

In the oldest parts of the town can be seen Romanesque and Gothic structures and many buildings from the 16th and 17th c. Especially interesting are those in Škor Square and at the end of Zadar Street, Politeo House from the 17th c. with a high courtyard wall, Bučić-Machiedo House, the renaissance Vranković-Carić House on Ploče, etc.

The parish church of St. Stephen (Sveti Stjepan) was built in 1605 on the site of an earlier church of the same name. With its façade, small forecourt and bell tower the structure gives a highly harmonious impression. Inside the building a baptismal font from the old church dating from 1592. Apart from an attractive choir the church houses a lovely triptych by Francesco de Santacroce (Madonna, Hieronymus, St. John the Baptist) which is more beautiful than the paintings of the same master in the Franciscan church in the town of Hvar.

The church of St. Nicholas (Sveti Nikola) on the road to the cemetery contains sculptures by Antonio Porri (Venetian art) and votive paintings contributed by local seamen. Adjoining the church there is a site where a woman ascetic was walled in alive according to her own wish (16th c.).

The former church of St. Hieronymus (Sveti Jerolim) near the swimming beach — once part of a hospice erected by Glagolithic monks — is a very interesting architectural structure.

The Dominican Monastery — founded in 1482 and fortified in the 16th c., has towers at the corners and a campanile similar to that of the church of St. Krševan in Zadar. A new church was built in 1893, but its exaggerated dimensions have spoiled the harmony of the architectural group as a whole.

In front of the main altar of the old church was the grave of Petar Hektorović, the great Croatian poet and builder of Tvrdalj.

The church contains several interesting paintings: St. Dominic with the Saints by an unidentified artist; St. Hyacinthe by Baldissero D'Anna, a follower of Palma jun.; and a lovely Christ's Burial by the great Venetian painter Jacopo Robusti Tintoretto (1512—1594). The old man in the painting is the poet Petar Hektorović, the donator, and the young woman his daughter Lucretia. On the main altar there is a wooden crucifix by a local artist of the 17th c. and a small, beautifully executed Venetian crucifix from 1703 by Giacomo Piazetto.

Above the monastery's *lapidarium* (collection of fragments of stone architecture) a large library and a collection of paintings including portraits of local personalities, paintings of old ships, a Pietà and a Madonna among Saints by G. B. Crespi, etc.

Tvrdalj — the fortified summer residence of the poet Petar Hektorović. Most of the large structure (length of front 60 m) is still well preserved. In building this residence (1520—1569) the poet was as much under the influence of considerations of defence as of those of leisure for himself and his friends as was the custom of European renaissance society. He therefore put the following inscription above the entrance to the garden with the fishpond: PETRUS HECTOREUS MARINI FILIUS PROPRIO SUMPTU ET INDUSTRIA AD SUUM ET AMICORUM USUM CONSTRUXIT (Built by Petrus Hectoreus, son of Marinus, by his own wealth and diligence to serve himself and his friends). A special feature of the building are the many witty inscriptions in both Latin and Croatian. The latter are the oldest Croatian inscriptions to be found on the island.

The fishpond looks as it did during the poet's lifetime: carefully tended with healthy, well-fed fishes. The garden has retained its original lay-out, but the interior of the house, apart from the vestibule, has changed its original appearance.

One of the wings of Tvrdalj houses the **Ethnographical Collection**. The **Nautical Collection** (in Biankini House) contains a library, the archives of the Stari Grad port authorities, portraits of famous Hvar sea captains, models of old sailing ships, old guns used in defence against pirates, etc.

The Art Collection contains works of many prominent artists including Ivan Meštrović (1883—1962), Juraj Plančić (1899—1930), the contemporary painter Bartol Petrić of Stari Grad, etc. The collection can be seen in Biankini House. Two other works of art worth mentioning are Hektorović's bust by Ivan Mirković (1956) in front of Tvrdalj, and the monument to National Liberation fighters by K. A. Radovani at Priko.

THROUGH HVAR'S PLAIN AND FOOTHILLS

The centre of the island and an important source of its wealth is an area of about 1,000 hectares of arable land. It stretches in a south-easterly direction from Stari Grad to Vrboska and is linked across the low pass at Vrbanja (the higher peak is called Gorica) with a smaller valley which extends from Svirče to Jelsa and is intersected by a brook (Sveta Mandalina) which fills with water during the rainy period.

The original Greek settlement Pharos, now Stari Grad, stood on the western edge of the valley, which contained farms of varying size, — first Illyrian then Greek and finally Roman — of which numerous traces of a material and linguistic nature have been preserved. Through the valley runs the Stari Grad-Jelsa road (10 km) with the road for Vrboska branching off at the parish church in Vrbanja. The villages Pitve and Vrisnik have their own road links with Jelsa and are connected with the main road by the Vrisnik-Svirče local road.

Old Slavs from the Neretva valley probably found the villages Pitve (Illyrian Pityeia) and Dol already inhabited because in the early Middle Ages the island's sparse population had taken refuge there on account of the ease with which these places could be defended.

Vrbanj was founded by Slavs from the Neretva valley. They did not settle the whole valley at once but founded village after village, first on a tribal basis and later on through the action of feudal lords.

Thus Vrbanj subsequently brought into being the villages Svirče and Vrboska (15th c.) while Pitve supplied the settlers for Vrisnik and Jelsa (14th c.).

Round these villages grow the island's most beautiful vineyards, and the whole valley is fresh and green with lush vegetation occasionally interspersed with olive trees some of which are more than a thousand years old. **Dol** stands in an area of the valley which was inhabited in ancient times. The village consists of two parts separated by a low hill crowned by the new church of St. Michael (Sveti Mihovil). A renovated 17th-century altar piece in the church shows highly realistic figures of local inhabitants walking in procession.

The church of St. Peter (Sveti Petar) in the western part of the village **(Dol Svete Marije)** has an interesting bell tower and a beautiful baroque wrought-iron screen enclosing the apse which contains a secession-style altar by Ivan Rendić, the first notable sculptor in Croatian modern art (1849—1932). On the altar a late-15th-century Madonna by an Italian painter known as Maestro di Stratonice (after one of his works), a follower of Sandro Botticelli.

The baroque church of St. Barbara in the other part of the village **(Dol Svete Barbare)** was recorded as early as 1226.

Vrbanj is the largest village on the island, the centre of popular uprisings (especially that of 1510), and the birthplace of Matija Ivanić. Dominating most of the Hvar plain, the village has a square, many ethnographically interesting details, and houses with defence walls and loopholes from the 16th and, especially, the 17th c. when the danger of pirate attack was at its height.

Of special interest is the house called Kraljevi dvori (the King's Palace) which dates from the Middle Ages and was a patrician residence, perhaps even the residence of a *župan* before 1278. Tradition attributes it wrongly to Matija Ivanić himself.

The parish church of the Holy Spirit (Sveti Duh; consecrated in 1793) stands on the site of an older church from the 15th c. The Descent of the Holy Spirit on the main altar is by Baldissero d'Anna whose works can also be seen in Stari Grad (monastery) and Sveta Nedjelja. The church also contains beautiful old ceremonial candelabra.

Above the village raise the ruins of the very old Romanesque church of St. Vitus (Sveti Vid) which is mentioned in a document from 1395.

The highest peak of the island (626 m) is surmounted by the chapel of St. Nicholas (Sveti Nikola) which was built by a group of seamen led by Matija Ivanić in demonstration of their own strength 23 years before the outbreak of the great rebellion. The document on the foundation of the chapel dates from 1487.

Svirče stands partly in the valley and partly on the lower southern slopes of Gorica hill. Its attractions include the church of St. Magdalene (20th c.), which replaced an old church from the 18th c. but retained its bell tower, and an old cemetery with cyprus trees (19th c.) which is protected as a historical monument. Especially interesting, both architecturally and ethnographically, are the old part of the village, the Carić houses which are linked together with small bridges, and the old residence of the patrician family Šimunić which played a prominent role from the 16th to the early 19th c. Protected by a wall, the residence houses nice specimens of halberds and the crown of a well with the inscription RADO SIMONI FECIT MDL. Below the house a mediaeval shepherd's dwelling dating from the same period as Kraljevi dvori.

The chapel of St. Mary (Sveta Marija) in the square, built about 1820 on the site of the former village loggia, has an interesting rustic choir. In the house of the self-taught sculptor Josip Makjanić (1837—1929) can be seen a collection of wood carvings.

Svirče is an outstanding example of urban architecture in rural Hvar.

Vrisnik — on a hill below the central ridge of the island, derives its name from the word *vrijes* (Croatian for 'heather'). Architecturally interesting is the Bojanić group of houses with its interlinking bridges and vaults which stands on the slope facing Svirče from where one obtains a beautiful panoramic view of the whole area.

Another vantage point is the elevated site of the parish church of St. Anthony the Abbot with its rows of old cypress trees and St. Roch's chapel. Nearby is the church of St. Dorothea (Sveta Doroteja).

Pitve — below a slope (Kaštil) of Samotorac hill commands the approach to the low Vratnik pass. Founded in ancient times (Illyrian Pityeia, recorded by Appolonius of Rhodos in the 3rd c. B.C.), the village has preserved a long continuity because of its outstanding defensive position. There also exists a younger settlement (from the 15th c.) called Novo Pitve (till the end of the 19th c. called Ostrvica) which — viewed from the north or the south — looks like an old castle because its houses are closely interlinked. Its founders were refugees who, led by a man called Duboković, fled from the mainland before the Turks after the fall of Bosnia (1463). The church of St. Jacob on a slope between the two settlements was built in 1877 to replace an older church from 1452. The site has been used for sacral purposes ever since ancient times. A head of Janus, the two-faced Roman deity, has survived in front of the church.

Through **Vratnik** pass runs an ancient winding road which ascends to a height of 550 m (Sveti Ante pass) before reaching the village of Zavala on the southern coast of the island. Within the pass begins a massive channel constructed in 1905 to collect surplus rain water from the mountains. Through the road tunnel (1,400 m long) leading from Vratnik to the southern coast of the island (Zavala, Ivandolac, Sveta Nedjelja) runs the water-supply system for the town of Hvar.

VRBOSKA

Vrboska is situated on a narrow channel extending inland from a wide and well protected bay on the northern coast of the island. The oscillations of the water in the channel (known as *šćiga*) forecast changes in the weather thus performing the function of both barometer and thermometer. The village offers an unusual sight on a karst island: houses rising on both shores of a channel spanned by several small bridges. In the channel itself, in the centre of the village, stands an islet (342 sq. m) with a monument to fallen fighters of the National Liberation War. A whole network of walking paths lead under the thick shade of pine-trees down to the swimming beaches. Beyond the channel the bay widens towards Jelsa in the south-east (40 min. away) and Glavica promontory in the north.

Vrboska has sea links with Split and road links with Jelsa and, via Vrbanja, with Stari Grad and Hvar.

The village came into existence in the 15th c. as the harbour of Vrbanja (*vallis Varbagni*).

The oldest houses dating from the 15th c. are of Gothic style or have Gothic ornaments. Some of them still show traces of devastating fire, — a reminder of the fights during the popular uprising (1510—1514) and of the Turkish naval attack and devastation in August 1571.

The original development of the harbour began in 1465 due to the efforts of the popular leader and local ship-owner Matija Ivanić, who kept a ship in Vrboska and built a house there in 1468 (on the southern shore of the channel).

A special attraction of Vrboska is its monumental church of St. Mary (15th c.) which was fortified about 1575. The renaissance structure occupies a large site and is a unique specimen of its kind on the Adriatic. The paintings which decorated the church are temporarily kept in the other parish church in order to protect them against dampness. The roof structure of the church surrounded by a crenellated wall is a good vantage point for a breathtaking view towards the mountains in the south and towards the east and the open sea. The original memorial tablets within the church still survive. The graves, marked with beautiful baroque numbers, include also several graves of commoners. A grave in the apse bears the coat-of-arms of parson Petar Fabrio from 1737 and the inscription NE DIFFERAS AMICE — HODIE MIHI CRAS TIBI (You won't be different, friend — Me today, you tomorrow).

The church of St. Laurence (Sveti Lovrinc) was also built in the 15th c. but has been twice enlarged, —

in the 16th and again in the 17th c. when it acquired its present baroque appearance and the beautiful baroque choir.

The chapel of St. Peter (Sveti Petar) on the waterfront was once under the patronship of the patrician family Hranotić who reconstructed it in 1469. According to the statute of the commune (1331) the chapel marked the shore end of the border between the ancient regions of Pitve and Vrbanj at a time when neither Vrboska nor Jelsa yet existed.

The channel with the small bridges, the renaissance and baroque houses in the Padva area (western end of the northern shore of the channel), the narrow streets around Pjaca, the lovely pine-wood and the general impression of protection and security lend Vrboska a peculiar charm of its own.

The churches of Vrboska house the greatest cultural treasures of the island of Hvar.

On the main altar of the church of St. Laurence stands a beautiful polyptych with the figures of St. Laurence, St. John the Baptist and St. Nicholas, and two miniatures below the large paintings. The masterly execution of the painting and the expression on the faces of the three saints, which is free of any pathos, indicate the greatness of the artist who is believed to have been Paolo Veronese (1528—1588), while according to local tradition it was painted by the great Tiziano Vecelli (1477—1576).

The church further houses a Madonna with Medallions by Leandro Bassano, three works of the Dubrovnik painter Celestin Medović (1869—1921), a silver cross with saints' figures by Tiziano Aspetti (about 1600), old church vestments and lace (17th c.), a Tyrolean Way of the Cross, and several votive offerings from local sea captains from the 19th c.

The paintings belonging to the fortified church of St. Mary include the following: Birth of St. Mary by Antonio Sciuri (1627), two works of Jacopo Alabardi (1590—1650), a Group of Saints by K. Zana from 1650, Our Lady of Mt. Carmel by S. Celesti (1659), — all works from Venetian schools of painting. The second painting Our Lady of Mt. Carmel is the work of the contemporary Dubrovnik painter Marko Rašica (b. 1883). There is also a small icon of local production dating from the 16th c.

JELSA

Jelsa was founded in the 14th c. as the port of the village of Pitve. The name derives from *jolhe,* the Croatian word for alder-trees which usually grow on ground rich in springs. Jelsa is still dominated by tall poplar trees, — an unusual sight for a Dalmatian island.

Approaching the place, one will feel the freshness of the woods covering the surrounding slopes. Facing towards Mt. Biokovo on the mainland, Jelsa seems to rise on the shore of one of the large Swiss lakes.

At first sight Jelsa seems a new place. The houses on the water front do not present façades of stone covered by century-old patina nor are they typical in design but rather point to the 19th c., the period of the greatest prosperity of the local shipping industry. The municipal park gives the village a modern touch.

Gradually, however, one discovers Jelsa's more distant past. Monuments from the classical period remain hidden, and so we shall not describe the Roman villas at Kutac and Sveti Rok. In the courtyard of the church can be seen a collection of stone fragments from different periods, including the gravestones of the Roman citizen

C. Val. Pompeianus, a Pietà from the 15th c., the upper part of a massive stone table from Obradić-Machiedo House from the 17th c., the Croatian inscription on a stone cross from the 17th c. (TACHO BUDI SVACHOME CHI POSISE NA BRATA SVOEGA — Let this be the fate of anybody who raises his hand against his own brother).

Before the mid-19th c. Jelsa had no built-up quayside, and the main line of communication ran behind the houses now lining the waterfront. In Sveti Ivan Square there are several houses of local citizens from the 16th c. onwards. A few renaissance buildings have survived as has also the portal of Skrivanelli House (behind the church) with a coat-of-arms, the year MDLXI and the inscription: DOMINUS CHUSTODIAT INTROITUM TUM ET EXITUM TUM (May the Lord guard thy entrance and thy exit). Running eastwards from the square can be seen houses from the 16th and 18th c. Specially worth mentioning is the house of Count Kačić Dimitri which has a massive façade, an ornamented side door, and a garden of classical design. Two streets lead from the square towards the west — one to the quay-side, the other (ulica Svetog Ivana) to the town's main square with the Slatina brook (regulated in 1847). The church (recorded in 1331) was fortified in 1535 and could successfully defend the place from Turkish attack in August 1571. The modern façade and the bell tower, added at the end of the 19th c., have considerably spoiled the otherwise beautiful renaissance structure (the original façade can be seen in a 17th-century painting within the church). The graves in the apse were damaged when its floor was covered with tiles in 1895. In the aisles, however, the graves of old local brotherhoods and crafts-men's families from the 16th c. still survive. The wooden statue of the Madonna on the main altar was brought

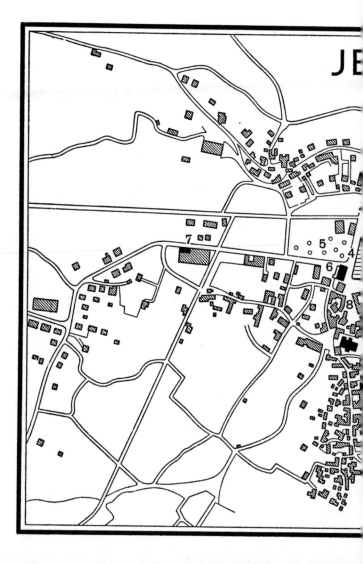

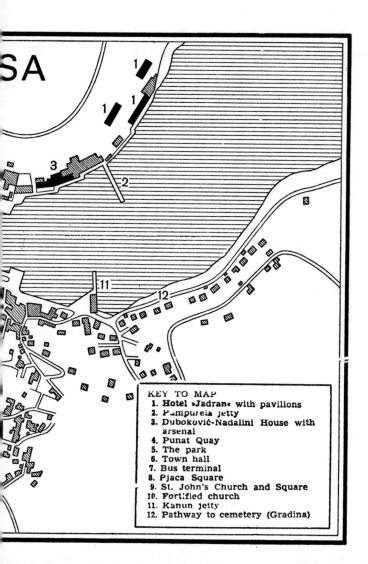

SA

KEY TO MAP
1. Hotel »Jadran« with pavilions
2. Pampurela jetty
3. Duboković-Nadalini House with
   arsenal
4. Punat Quay
5. The park
6. Town hall
7. Bus terminal
8. Pjaca Square
9. St. John's Church and Square
10. Fortified church
11. Kanun jetty
12. Pathway to cemetery (Gradina)

here from the Sinj region on the mainland in 1539 by refugees fleeing before the Turks. The statue is celebrated every year on St. Mary's Day (25 August — Gospa Stomorena).

The sacristy houses a collection of church vestments, liturgical vessels, valuable crucifixes, etc.

The painting of the Madonna with St. Fabian and St. Sebastian in the large southern chapel is a work of the Flemish-Venetian painter Pieter de Costera (1612/14—1704).

A large plaque on the new building of the grammar school erected to the memory of 107 fallen fighters of the National Liberation War bears the following verses (in translation):-

They were not present on the morning of triumph.

Immortal like freedom,

They built their lives

Into the foundations of freedom.

The harbour and the jetties began to be erected about 1830 when work was resumed on draining the boggy land separating the two parts of Jelsa (Vela Banda and Mala Banda) to create the present fertile plain called Solina which was planted with poplars in 1871. Part of Solina has been developed as a park, one of the most beautiful in Dalmatia.

On the top of the southern hill with the castle and the Slatina brook below stands the votive church of Our Lady (erected in 1535 and several times enlarged) with a bell tower from 1862 and a small wood planted in 1906. The district which is situated at the foot of the hill and is called Banski dolac contains several stylistically interesting houses. The entrance into Selem House in the main street of Banski dolac bears a Latin inscription from the 17th c. besides an analogous one in Croatian.

The path leading by the sea to the cemetery is recorded in the Statute of 1331. A branch path forks off towards Mina beach. The cemetery stands on the site of a former Augustinian monastery (founded in 1605; order dissolved in 1787). Only the church of the monastery has survived while the stone of the other buildings has been used for the erection of graves.

The cemetery is situated on a small promontory which was protected by a defence wall in the early Middle Ages. The wall can still be seen where it spans the peninsula at its narrowest part. Remains of even older defence walls which surrounded the whole peninsula were discovered by the sea a few years ago. By 1331 the peninsula was no longer a fortification and was already then called Gradina (= ruins).

In the surroundings of Jelsa there are two monuments of major archaelogical importance.

One of them is the megalithic structure known as Tor which perches on a slope below the island's ridge. Built on an earlier, Illyrian structure, Tor was once (4—5 c. B.C.) a strong Greek watch tower which commanded the whole of the Makarska Channel as far as the entrance to the Bay of Stari Grad. The other one, called Galešnik or Grad, which is situated slightly more to the east on an isolated cliff, is the ruins of an old fortress. The base of this structure is Illyrian and the superstructure Roman. In the early Middle Ages the fortress was still inhabited. Its present name — like that of the islet at the approach to Hvar harbour — is believed to derive from the nobleman Galeša Slavogosti who led an unsuccessful rebellion against Venice in 1310 using this fortification as his stronghold, and was forced to flee. The road leading to Grad is an old Roman road overlaying an older, Illyrian road.

Excursions from Jelsa

Jelsa is encircled by five villages: Pitve (about 40 min. walking), Vrisnik (60 min.), Svirče and Vrbanj (60 min. by the main road), and Vrboska (1 hour on a lovely path along the edge of the sea). On the road to Svirče, in the area known as Rake and south-west from a large karst field called Polanda, can be seen the highly interesting remains of a farm of the »Illyrian type«. Zavala, on the southern coast of the island, can be reached via Pitve through Vratnik pass and Sveti Antun pass (550 m) within 2 1/2 hours, or by car on the new road (6 km) through the Vratnik tunnel (Yugoslavia's longest road tunnel) within 20 minutes. From Zavala one can proceed to Ivandolac (4 km) and further on to Sveta Nedjelja (4 km).

The road from Jelsa to Sućuraj (51 km) is a continuation of the Hvar — Stari Grad — Jelsa road. After passing Mina beach immediately behind the cemetery of Jelsa we reach an historical area called Plame (in more recent times the name has applied only to the areas of Gdinj and Bogomolje). In the Middle Ages the area was inhabited chiefly by shepherds who lived in permanent or temporary dwellings. However, as early as in the 14th c. the first private holdings began to emerge in the coves Pogorila, Stiniva and Sveta Luka. During the Venetian-Turkish wars in the 17th c. many people fled from the mainland to the islands and many of the refugees settled in Hvar, especially in Plame. Hence the existing differences in dialect between the western and the eastern parts of the island. The language border is in the village of Bogomolje.

The chapel of St. Luke (Sveti Luka) east of Jelsa stands in an archaelogical locality. By the sea the remains of a Roman villa. The chapel was built under the patronage of the island's oldest patrician family in the 14th c., but was subsequently enlarged. The altar is in baroque style.

Gornja Prapatna — a small village with ethnographically interesting houses in rustic style, old bread ovens, oil presses, etc. Below the road, an ancient path leads to Prapatna Cove with the summer residence of the patrician family Angelini from the 18th c. The building is completely rustic in style without any urban elements. In the hills south of Gornja Prapatna the tiny old village of **Humac** which developed from temporary dwellings of shepherds in the 15th and 16th c. A 30-minute walk southwards from Humac (in the company of a guide) brings us to the prehistoric cave known as **Gračeva špilja** which stands at the head of a small ravine below the top of the hill. Archaeologically this is the island's most interesting cave, for traces of a culture from the 3rd millennium B.C. have been discovered here. Thus life in Hvar may be said to cover a series of cultures over a time span of 5,000 years. The cave can also be reached from Jelsa (4 hours' walk) by the old road for Galešnik, or from Gromindolac on the southern coast. Below the cave down by the sea is a fresh-water spring called Virak.

Findings from this cave and from Markova špilja can be seen in the archaeological collection of the Dominican church of St. Mark (Sveti Marko) in Hvar.

Poljica — the first village to be reached on the Jelsa-Sućuraj road, is a comparatively new and very clean settlement. Below the village and the road the coves **Mala Stiniva** and **Vela Stiniva.**

In Vela Stiniva can be seen the summer residence of the patrician family Angelini (later Duboković-Nadalini) from the 18th c., — a modest specimen of the local baroque style.

From Poljica we reach the village of **Zastražišće** which guarded the approach to the Hvar plain. The original role of the village is indicated by its name which derives from the Croatian word *straža* which means »guard«. On the hill (Vela glava, 316 m) stand the remains of an Illyrian fortification dating from 1000 B.C.

The Hvar plain was also safe from surprise attack in Turkish times if the sea was watched from these vantage points.

Of the two former defence towers of the patrician family Angjelinović (one destroyed, the other completely reconstructed) only a Croatian inscription from 1624 has been preserved. The towers were designed primarily as protection against attacks by Turkish pirates. A climb to the parish church of St. Nicholas (Sveti Nikola) will be rewarded by a lovely view of Mt. Biokovo and the Dalmatican coast across the Hvar Channel.

The chapel of St. Barbara was erected on the site of an older structure from the 14th c. and reconstructed in 1621.

The village itself consists of four separate parts: Mala Banda with the church, Podstranje, Donje Poje and Grudac, all of which contain interesting specimens of rustic architecture.

In **Črvanj Cove** 30 minutes south from Zastražišće, a cluster of simple houses and the ruins of a patrician residence (first Angelini, later Duboković-Nadalini). On the northern coast and close by Zastražišće the attractive Dubac Cove.

About half-way on the road to Gdinj on the northern side of the island the twin coves of Pokarvenik (Pokrivenik) below imposing cliffs and another famous cave. The coves can now be approached on a good road branching off the main road (6 km from the crossroads). There is also a jetty for boats.

Gdinj — 21 km east of Zastražišće by the main road we first reach the part of Gdinj which is called Dugi Dolac (2 km from the centre of the village). The other parts of the village are called Nova Crkva, Stara Crkva, Visoka and Bonkovići (the latter on the southern slope of the hill, is marked by an interesting lay-out).

About 800 m north-east from the centre, in the shade of old cypress trees stands the 16th-century church of St. George (Sveti Juraj) with the old rectory built in renaissance and baroque style.

The fact that the church of St. Lucy (Sveta Lucija) was the patronate of the patrician Kašić as early as in 1599 suggests that Gdinj must have existed before that time (14th c. or before), probably as a settlement of shepherds. If we accept the etymological explanation that the name Gdinj derives from the word *bditi* (= to watch) then it is certain that the area was inhabited even in prehistoric times.

Judging by the monumental and picturesque ruins known as Vela gomila and several other remains which have only recently disappeared, the area was inhabited and played an important role during the Bronze Age (Illyrians).

In the centre of Gdinj a collection of books and paintings by Ivko Radovanović. On the road to Visoka a graceful pyramid erected to the memory of fallen National Liberation fighters.

In the part of Gdinj called Visoka there are interesting old houses: Visković Houses with their old balconies and courtyard, rustic houses in Kola Street built without the use of mortar, old shepherds' shelters, and numerous interesting ethnographical features.

On the southern side of the island, descending through a steep ravine past century-old cypress trees, we reach

Smreka Cove (45 min. from Gdinj). In the cove another summer residence of the Angelini family with a house chapel and defences against pirate attack.

In a smaller cove (Kožija) west of Smreka, the tower of Count Matija Bartulović from 1700, also designed for protection against pirate attack.

Likova glava (417 m) near Gdinj is the last in the chain of hills extending eastwards from Zastražišće. From here the ground gradually slopes down towards Sućuraj (Sveti Nikola, 168 m) allowing a wide view towards Bogomolje, with Mt Biokovo on the left-hand side across the sea rising to giant proportions like the high bank of a huge river which the Hvar Channel resembles in this place.

East of Gdinj in the valley, the village of **Bogomolje** which consists of four parts each comprising a cluster of houses: Srid Sela, Glava, Rače Njiva and Jerkov dvor. The inhabitants use both dialects, but the continental mentality and manner of dressing prevail.

The tiny baroque parish church (1605) has a façade from 1750 and is surrounded by graves. There is an interesting old kitchen and ante-room in the house of Mirko Barbanić. The monument to fallen fighters of the National Liberation War in the main square is by Joko Knežević.

The village harbour (Bogomolja Bristova) is on the northern side of the island about 3 km away.

The road from Bogomolja to Sućuraj (18 km) passes through Marijin dvor and Jerkovići which together with Zaglav on the southern side of the island make up Selca Bogomoljska.

Zaglav is an interesting primitive settlement in a wild natural setting with caves containing traces of old cultures (stairs cut in rock in the cave). 2.5 km before

Sućuraj the ground descends to an altitude of only 25 m emphasizing still more the massive bulk of Mt. Biokovo on the mainland coast.

Sućuraj derives its name from the original church of St. George (Sveti Juraj) which was recorded as early as in 1331. The present building dates from the late 19th c. Remains of shepherds' (and perhaps fishermen's) dwellings from the 14th c. have been found round the church. By the 16th c. the village had 150 inhabitants, and Augustinian monks had already arrived to take over parish functions (1573).

The danger of attack by pirates from the Neretva valley in Turkish times led to the construction of interlinked groups of houses and the erection of gates at street entrances (e. g. Modrići).

The demographic division of the population which resulted from the arrival of refugees from the mainland who were fleeing before the Turks during repeated outbreaks of war in the 17th c. (Cretan war 1645—1669, Morean war 1684—1699) influenced the development of the place, the original inhabitants remaining on the northern side of the harbour and the newcomers settling on the southern side (Gornja Banda, and Donja Banda). The architecture of the village suffered greatly during the Second World War. The rectory is the former Augustinian monastery (the order was abolished in 1787). The church of St. Anthony (Sveti Antun) in Donja Banda, founded by Franciscan monks in 1633, contains a collection of fragments of stone architecture *(lapidarium)*. The new parish church of St. George (Sveti Juraj) dates from the end of the 19th c. In the porch (once an old and much smaller structure) can be seen a grave inscription in Cyrillic letters which points to the continental descent of part of the inhabitants.

In one of the now empty graves of the old church lay the body of Bishop Bartol Kačić, the spiritual leader of the people during the wars of the period, who after fleeing from Makarska settled in Sućuraj and died there in 1645. Next to him lay his brother Count Petar Kačić Žarković. The modest sacristy houses two historical chalices: one was a present of Pope Gregor XV to Bishop Bartol (about 1621) and the other was given to the church by the French Duke d'Alençon (1844—1910).

In the school garden stands a monument to fallen National Liberation fighters erected in 1966.

Both shores of this narrow neck of the island, between Gdinj and Bogomolje and further on to Sućuraj, contain numerous attractive coves and beaches of which only the largest have been mentioned. The following is a list of those which due to their natural attractions have been proclaimed protected natural areas: Mlaska (as far as Sućuraj), Krivodolac, Studenac, Divlja Vela, Divlja Mala, Gornja Didina, Donja Didina, Mala Mosevčica, Vela Mosevčica — on the northern coast, and on the southern: Perna, Židigova, Rasohatica, Slivanske Lučice, Prapatna, Martinovik (mooring place) and Aržišće.

HOTELS, CAMPS FOR MOTORISTS AND RESTAURANTS

Hvar

Hotels

The Hvar Hotel Enterprise controls the following hotels:

»Adriatic« (A category) — 126 beds, Tel. 74-024

»Amfora« (A cat.) — 768 beds. Large, well-equipped in-door swimming-pool with stands for national and international sports competitions in swimming, waterpolo etc., a hall for gymnastic tournaments and training and for various kinds of ball game, a physiotherapeutic section, a hall for lectures and symposiums, and facilities for film projections. Tel. 74-202

»Palace« (A cat. — 140 beds) built in 1903 but now completely renovated and provided with modern equipment. The hotel's premises include the old City Loggia, an outstanding specimen of Dalmatian architecture from Venetian times. Tel. 74-013

»Bodul« (B cat.) — 300 beds, Tel. 74-049

»Dalmacija« (B cat.) — 130 beds, Tel. 74-120

»Galeb« (B cat.) — 115 beds, Tel. 74-044

»Pharos« (B cat.) — 335 beds, Tel. 74-028

»Sirena« (B cat.) — 316 beds, Tel. 74-104

»Delfin« (B cat.) — 110 beds, Tel. 74-168

All Hvar hotels are provided with central heating equipment while hotels of A category include in-door swimming-pools with sea water which are open throughout the year.

In co-operation with the Yugoslav Academy of Science and Art the Hvar Hotel Enterprise opened in 1973 a Medical Centre for Allergies with a bay hospital thus giving Hvar, as a prominent climatic resort, suitable therapeutic facilities run by prominent medical experts. The Castle (locally called *fortica*) has been most successfully reconstructed as a recreation centre with a small hotel, a restaurant, bar, night club and several terraces which command a lovely view of the town and the sea. Floodlit at night, the castle and the municipal square, the water front and the town's prominent cultural monuments (the Cathedral, the Franciscan Monastery, the Arsenal) offer a most impressive view.

Starigrad

Hotels

The »**Helios**« hotel settlement (B cat., Tel. 75-822, 4 pavilions, 428 beds) has a central reception desk and a large restaurant with a terrace for dancing, and a disk club.

»**Bungalows**« — 108 beds which can be rented with the use of kitchen or only as accommodation with meals at the »Helios« central restaurant.

Hotel »**Adriatic**« — 175 beds, restaurant and TV room, private beach, mini-golf, children's playground, table-tennis, two tennis courts, etc.

The FKK beach at Zavala includes a refreshment pavilion.

Accommodation facilities in the town

Hotel »**Jadran**« (C cat., 33 beds, Tel. 75-827), with restaurant seating 300, and a comfortable terrace.

»**Bungalows**«, »**Jurjevac**« camp — 132 beds

Camping tents for 362 persons

Camping site

»Stari Grad« camp — Information: Hotelsko poduzeće »Helios«, Tel. 75-822

Restaurants

»**Gradski restoran**«

»**Tri palme**«

»**Expresso**«

Pub in the harbour

The hotels organize excursions by private boats to neighbouring coves (sea food, grilled meat and drinks provided) and to Hvar and Bol.

Jelsa

Hotels

»Jadran« (B. cat., 4 buildings). Open from 1 May — 31 Oct. Address: 58465 Jelsa, Tel. 75-615, cables: JADRAN JELSA. 146 bedroms (28 single) with 274 beds. Restaurants. 350 m from the centre of Jelsa, 50 m from the beach.

»Fontana« (ex Genex) (B cat., 15 pavilions). Open from 1 May — 31 Oct. Addr.: 58465 Jelsa. Tel. 75-632, cables: FONTANA — JELSA. 160 bedrooms with 276 beds (no single bedrooms). 800 m from the centre, 100 m from the beach.

»Mina« (B cat.). Open from 1 Jan — 31. Dec. Address: 58465 Jelsa. Tel. 75-607/74-320, cables: MINA — JELSA, 199 bedrooms (20 single) with 393 beds. Restaurants. 800 m from the centre, 50 m from the beach.

Camping sites

»Mina« camp — Information: Komunalno poduzeće, Jelsa, Tel. 75-627

»Holiday« camp — Information: Privredno poduzeće, Jelsa

Vrboska

Hotels

»Adriatic« (B cat., 4 buildings). Open from 15 Apr — 31 Oct. Address: 58465 Jelsa — Vrboska. Tel. 75-433, cables: ADRIATIC — JELSA. 188 bedrooms (18 single) with 358 beds, restaurants. 1,500 m from Vrboska, 1 sea mile from Jelsa, 50 m from the swimming beach.

»Madeira« (C cat.) open from 1 May — 31 Oct. Address: 58465 MADEIRA, Jelsa — Vrboska. Tel. 75-415, cables:

MADEIRA VRBOSKA — JELSA. 20 bedrooms (4 triple, 16 double), restaurant. 100 m from Vrboska, 20 m from the beach.

Camping site

»Auto-camp Vrboska« — Information: Turistički biro, Tel. 75-403

Sućuraj

Hotel **»Perna«** (B cat.), 80 beds. Tel. No. 6

TOURIST AGENCIES

Tourist agencies apart from offering regular tourist services organize excursions to Dubrovnik, Mostar, Korčula and Biševo.

Hvar

»Atlas« — Tel. 74-087
»Dalmacijaturist« — Tel. 74-021 and 74-105
»Turist biro« — Tel. 74-132 and 74-036

Stari Grad

»Dalmacijaturist« — Tel. 75-825
Central reception desk Hotel **»Helios«** for private accommodation — Tel. 75-821

Jelsa

»Atlas« — Tel. 75-645
»Dalmacijaturist« — Tel. 75-606
»Turistička agencija« — Tel. 75-628

PETROL STATIONS

Hvar

INA petrol station, Tel. 74-160, open (in summer) from 6 a.m. till 10 p.m.

Jelsa

INA petrol station, Tel. 75-648, open (in summer) from 6 a.m. till 10 p.m.

MEDICAL INSTITUTIONS

Hvar

Emergency ward, Tel. 74-111
Medical Centre for Allergies, Tel. 74-151

Starigrad

Emergency ward, Tel. 75-805

Jelsa

Emergency ward, Tel. 75-602

Vrboska

Emergency ward, Tel. 75-404

CONTENTS

Prema mišljenju Republ. sekret. za prosvj., kult. i fiz. kult. SRH br. 915/1-1973. od 21. II 73. ova se knjiga smatra proizvodom iz člana 36. stav 1. točka 7 Zakona o oporezivanju proizvoda i usluga i na nju se ne plaća porez na promet.

Printed by: AZUR, Zagreb — »Narodni list«, Zadar